THE AMAZING APPLE BOOK

Written by
Paulette Bourgeois

Illustrated by
Linda Hendry

Addison-Wesley Publishing Company, Inc.
Reading, Massachusetts   Menlo Park, California   New York
Don Mills, Ontario   Wokingham, England   Amsterdam   Bonn
Sydney   Singapore   Tokyo   Madrid   San Juan

To the first apples of my eye,
my parents, Matt and Freda.

Acknowledgments

This book was possible because of the generous information provided by the Ontario Apple Marketing Commission, the Ontario Ministry of Agriculture and Food, the British Columbia Ministry of Agriculture and Food and the Agriculture Departments of the provinces of New Brunswick and Nova Scotia. I am grateful for reference help from the librarians at many of the Metropolitan Toronto public libraries. I would like to thank the Food Advisory Division of Agriculture Canada for giving permission to adapt and reprint their recipes. Dr. John Proctor kindly read the manuscript and made sure that I knew my stamens from my pistils. And, finally, thank you to Ricky, Rob, Val and Valerie at Kids Can Press for their ideas, editing skills and support.

Library of Congress Cataloging-in-Publication Data

Bourgeois, Paulette.
    The amazing apple book / written by Paulette Bourgeois ; illustrated by Linda Hendry.
       p. cm.
    Summary: Describes, in simple text and illustrations, the history, cultivation, and many uses of apples.
    ISBN 0-201-52333-7
    1. Apple — Juvenile literature. [1. Apple.] I. Hendry, Linda, ill. II. Title.
SB363.B68 1990
641.3′411 — dc20   89-28070
                                                     CIP

Edited by Valerie Wyatt
Book design by Michael Solomon
Set in 13-point Century Schoolbook by Imprint Typesetting, Canada

ABCDEFGHIJ–AL–89
First printing, January 1990

Contents

What keeps you healthy, cleans your teeth and goes munch, munch, crunch, crunch?

Need more clues? What can you boil, bake, broil, press, pickle and dry to a shrivelled leather?

Give up? It's an apple!

When you read *The Amazing Apple Book* you'll discover why an apple tree and a raspberry bush are cousins. You'll find out how Johnny Appleseed got his name and learn why we don't grow apple trees from seeds. You'll find facts and figures,

fun and games. And there are some truly terrible riddles.

Here's one to get you going:

Q. What book can you read until the end and not quite finish?

A. *The Amazing Apple Book,* because after you've finished reading it there's still lots to do — like making apple dolls and whipping up blue candy apples.

P.S. Whenever you see a word that is printed in dark letters like **this**, you will find the word described in the Glossary at the back of the book.

An apple family tree

Take a look at the people in your family. Chances are that even though you are related you all look different. Perhaps you are blond and skinny while your cousin is dark and plump. Maybe your uncle is so short that he has to stretch to reach the kitchen cupboards while your grandmother is so tall that she has to duck every time she goes through a doorway. But because you are a family you have many things in common. You share common ancestors.

As a human being, you're also part of a bigger family—the mammal family. Your mammal "cousins" include whales and apes.

Plants have families too. And as in human families, there are lots of varieties. Apples can be red, small, hard and sour, and they can be green, plump, juicy and deliciously sweet. In all there are about 7,000 different kinds of apples.

Like humans, apples are also part of a larger family—the rose family. Their rose cousins include peaches, plums, pears, almonds, raspberries, strawberries, cherries and apricots. The members of the rose family have some things in common. All have flowers with five petals and five **sepals**.

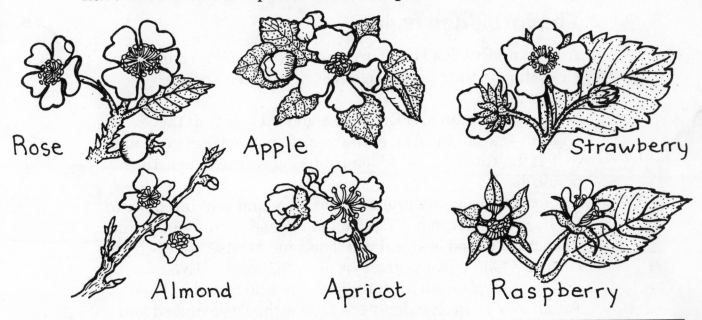

Rose   Apple   Strawberry

Almond   Apricot   Raspberry

Candy?
No thanks. I like roses better.
It may seem odd that you can eat apples, raspberries, cherries and almonds—everything but the roses from the rose family. But—surprise—you can eat roses! Some people eat the petals in salads. And many people enjoy rose hip tea made from the **fruit** of the rose. The rose hip is bursting with Vitamin C. During World War II soldiers drank rose hip tea to stay healthy.

The apple through history

Many, many storytellers have woven tales of mystery, romance and wonder around the apple. One of the best-known apple stories is in the Bible. It is the story of Adam and Eve, who are said to be the first man and woman in the world.

The forbidden fruit

Adam and Eve lived in a paradise called the Garden of Eden. Even though they wore no clothes, they weren't cold or embarrassed.

God told Adam and Eve they could eat any fruit they wished—except the fruit of the tree of knowledge of good and evil. If they ate that forbidden fruit, God warned them, they would die.

One day a snake slithered beside Eve and convinced her to try the forbidden fruit. "The fruit isn't deadly," the snake said. "The truth is God is afraid you'll become as wise as he is if you eat some. God is just trying to scare you." And so Eve picked an apple from the forbidden tree and tasted it. Then Adam took a bite. Suddenly they knew they were naked and they were ashamed. They made themselves clothes from fig leaves and hid from God.

God soon found Adam and Eve. They told Him they were ashamed of their nakedness. And then God knew that Adam and Eve had eaten some of the forbidden fruit. Eve told God that the snake had tricked her. And God was angry and told the snake that forever more it would have to crawl on its belly eating dust. God made coats for Adam and Eve and told them they must leave the Garden of Eden forever.

The golden apples

There are many tales and legends about apples. Remember how the wicked step-mother gave Snow White a poisoned apple? Another apple story tells how an apple caused a war between the people of Greece and Troy long ago. But one apple story you may not know is a Norse legend about a princess, three golden apples and a glass hill. The story goes like this:

NCE upon a time there was a farmer with three sons. Every year, on the night before the hay was cut, all the hay would disappear from the fields. Something was eating it! One year the farmer sent his oldest son to a barn beside the field to guard the hay. In the middle of the night the walls of the barn started to shake and the ground started rumbling and the son ran home terrified. In the morning, all the hay had been eaten. The same thing happened the next year to the second son.

The year after, the farmer sent his third son, Boots, to guard the hay. Boots wasn't very smart. He usually spent his time cleaning the fireplace. But when the rumbling and the clatter started, Boots stayed in the barn. Finally, it was silent. When Boots checked the fields, he found a horse starting to eat the hay. It wore a brass saddle and carried a full set of armour for a knight. Boots hid the horse in a stable and saved the hay.

The next year the same thing happened, but this time Boots found a horse with a silver saddle and a set of silver armour. The year after that, Boots stayed in the barn through the most ferocious earthquakes. Then he found a horse with a golden saddle and some golden armour!

Now in the same kingdom the king declared a challenge: whoever could get three apples from the king's daughter who was sitting on top of a glass hill could marry her and keep half the kingdom.

The first day, Boots's two brothers went to the race, but Boots had to stay home and clean the fireplace. Thousands of knights tried to climb the glass hill, but it was impossible. Then a knight in shiny brass armour appeared out of nowhere and managed to climb a third of the way up. The princess was so enchanted that she threw him a golden apple. But the knight rode away as mysteriously as he had come.

The next day Boots was once again told to stay home, and again the knights tried in vain to climb the hill. Out of the blue came a knight in brilliant silver armour. He climbed two-thirds of the way up the hill, and the princess tossed him a golden apple. Then he too rode away.

The next day when all the knights had failed, a knight dressed in gold rode to the top of the hill, plucked the third apple out of the princess's hand and rode away.

The king ordered everyone in the kingdom to appear at his castle. He wanted to find the knight with the golden apples. Everyone but Boots appeared. The king sent for him. Boots took three golden apples out of his pocket and threw off his sooty work clothes to reveal a suit of golden armour. The king gave Boots his daughter and half the kingdom. And they say nobody ever again climbed the hill of glass.

A straight shooter

William Tell was a real person who lived in Switzerland back in the fourteenth century when Austria was in control of the country. In every Swiss province there was an Austrian sheriff. One day in William Tell's town, the sheriff tried to humiliate all the townspeople by forcing them to bow to a hat perched on top of a pole. William Tell was big, strong and the best bow-and-arrow shooter anywhere. There was no way he would bow to a hat! He refused.

William Tell was arrested for disobeying. He was given a life or death challenge. The sheriff said if William Tell could shoot an arrow through an apple on top of a boy's head, he could go free. That boy was William Tell's own son!

The young boy stood bravely. Every muscle in his body was tight. He didn't shake. He knew he might die if the arrow missed. But he trusted his father.

William Tell hesitated. As he pulled the arrow taut, the boy smiled. William Tell sensed his son's trust and shot the arrow. It flew through the air with a *phhht* and cut through the apple.

Most people think the story ends here but it doesn't. William turned to the sheriff and said, "If my son had been hurt, I would have killed you." The bold marksman had gone too far. The sheriff had William Tell bound in chains and sentenced him to an island prison.

The lake was lashed by wild waves. The sheriff started rowing his prisoner to the island prison. The boat rocked wildly. Fearing that they would drown, the sheriff unlocked William Tell's chains and shouted: "Row!"

They battled the storm and landed, exhausted, on the island shore. They were safe, but only one man would survive. Someone had slipped Tell's bow and arrow into the boat. He shot the sheriff dead. From that time on, William Tell fought for the freedom of the Swiss people and became a hero. And all of *that* happened because of an apple.

Eureka!

One day Isaac Newton, an English scientist, was daydreaming under an apple tree. An apple fell to the ground and he found himself wondering: why do apples fall down? Why don't they fall up? Why do the stars and the moon stay in the sky?

An Italian scientist named Galileo had already discovered the answer. These things happened because of gravity, a force pulling every object in the universe toward every other object in the universe. Galileo also proved that falling objects (like Newton's apple) pick up speed as they fall. But Newton's observation of the falling apple did lead him to discover many more important things about gravity. For example, he discovered that the increase in falling speed is less when an apple (or any other object) is dropped from a great height.

Applexperiment

Here's some apple science you can
try for yourself.
You'll need:
a towel rack or other fixed horizontal bar, such as a
    swing set
two apples
two pieces of string about as long as your arm
1. Tie two apples from the bar so
they dangle 2 cm (1 inch) apart.
2. Challenge a friend to blow the
apples apart. It doesn't matter how
hard he or she tries, the apples will
never be blown apart. In fact they'll
be closer together.

Why? When your
friend blows, the air between the
apples is removed causing a low
pressure area. The air pressure
around the apples is more than the
pressure between them, so the
apples are forced together.

Two apple heroes

Our apples would be very different today if it hadn't been for two apple heroes from pioneer times — Johnny Appleseed and John McIntosh.

Johnny Appleseed

You might have thought that Johnny Appleseed was a storybook character. But he was a real person named John Chapman who was born in Massachusetts in pioneer times. Johnny was a gentle, religious man who loved animals and nature. He was afraid pruning would hurt a tree, and he never killed a mosquito or an ant! He was also very weird. He was terribly tall and skinny. He wore a pot on his head. When he didn't use it as a hat, he used it to cook dinner. He cut holes in coffee sacks and wore them as shirts. His pants were tattered around the bottom, and he wrapped rags around his feet instead of wearing shoes. Johnny always carried a handful of apple seeds and he planted them wherever he went.

Johnny was a hard-working loner. He didn't need much to make him happy — just some apple seeds or seedlings. He didn't even have a house. He slept on pine needles outdoors. Most of the time Johnny wandered along rutted pioneer wagon trails and paths made by the Native People, scattering apple seeds or starting small orchards. It wasn't long before settlers started to call him Johnny Appleseed. Today, many of the orchards in the Ohio Valley can be traced back to this odd wanderer.

John McIntosh

Whatever fruit store you walk into you are sure to see a familiar apple—it's as round as the moon with a fire-engine red skin and a juicy, sweet taste. It's the McIntosh, a favourite apple for eating and cooking. It's named after a Canadian pioneer farmer.

About the time that Johnny Appleseed was wandering the wild west, John McIntosh, the son of a Scottish farmer, was moving from his home in New York to start a farm in Upper Canada. He was clearing the land when he found some apple trees. He carefully uprooted the young trees and planted them in a garden beside his house.

Most of the trees produced apples that tasted terrible. They were soft or mushy or dry or bitter. But one tree had the juiciest, reddest apple that John McIntosh had ever seen. All of his neighbours wanted a taste. Soon word of this apple spread through Upper Canada and the apple became known as the McIntosh Red.

John McIntosh was happy to give away his apples but his son Allan had a better idea. He wanted to **graft** part of the tree onto other trees in the garden to start a McIntosh Red orchard. Soon many of the trees in the area were producing the famous apple. Allan McIntosh started selling seedlings and the rest is history.

Half of the original apple tree burned when the McIntosh farmhouse caught fire in 1894, but amazingly, the other half kept producing apples for another twelve years. Today, if you visit Dundela, Ontario, the place where McIntosh settled, you'll find a monument to the McIntosh Red.

All the animals in Noah's Ark came in pairs. Except the worms. They came in apples.

The apple in pioneer times

When pioneer settlers came to North America from England, France, Germany and Holland, they learned about surviving in the wilderness from the Native People. They taught the new arrivals about growing maize (corn), beans and vegetables. But it was the settlers who taught the Native People about apples.

Before the pioneers came, the only apples in North America were crab-apples. They tasted so sour that the Native People never ate them. The pioneers brought real apple tree seeds, seedlings and even small trees from their home countries and grew sweet apples. Not long after the Native People tasted this new fruit, they started planting orchards themselves.

Most pioneers had at least one apple tree in their yards. Many of the new farmers grew orchards with a hundred or more trees. In the beginning the farmers did not use **budding** and **grafting**; they let the trees grow naturally. This meant that the apple trees were all different and the orchards were called mixed orchards.

As soon as the pioneers found the land they would make their home, they planted apples. If they moved, they packed their treasures, their clothes, their furniture—and their seeds or seedlings for growing apple trees.

Apples everywhere

In 1625, the first apple orchard in America was planted by a minister in Boston. By 1644, John Endecott, governor of the Massachusetts Bay colony, owned more than 500 trees all by himself!

Everyone likes to eat apples but the pioneers *needed* apples.
They used apples for making juice, cider, apple butter,
dried apples, vinegar and food for the pigs, horses and cows.
There wasn't a part of the tree that the pioneers didn't use.
They whittled the wood to make parts for their machines and
children's toys. They even made furniture out of old apple
barrels and burned the gnarled roots of old trees for warmth.

Pioneer apples all year round

During the long harsh winters the pioneers had no way of getting fresh fruits and vegetables; there were no fridges or supermarkets stocked with oranges and grapefruits. But they did find ways to preserve some summer-grown fruits and vegetables, including apples. The most popular method of preserving food was to dry it.

Food goes bad when **bacteria** start to live on it. But bacteria need water to live. Although the settlers didn't know how bacteria multiplied, they knew that drying the food would stop it from rotting. The dried food didn't contain water, so the bacteria died.

In pioneer days everyone—moms, dads, kids, grandparents and neighbours—got together after the apples were picked in the fall for an apple-paring "bee." All day long they peeled, cored and sliced the apples. Then they dried the apples. There were different ways to do this.

In some places all the apple slices were laid out on a big net. The net was hung high off the ground between trees or posts. As the warm air moved over the apples, the water inside the fruit evaporated. Bees and flies sped up the drying by sucking the juices out of the fruit. If it didn't rain, the dried fruit was ready to store in pottery jars in two or three days.

In other places the pioneers hung the apples on strings to dry. You can try this at home. For instructions, see the box on the next page.

Apple drying was a good excuse to have a party. It was lots of hard work, but it gave the pioneers a chance to gossip and then celebrate with food and dancing.

During the winter the pioneers ate the dried apples as they were or soaked them in water and baked them into pies.

What is red, noisy and dangerous?

A stampeding herd of apples.

Make your own dried apples

You'll need:
a peeler
a small knife
a long piece of string
8 apples

1. Peel and core the apples as shown.
2. Turn the apples on their sides and cut them into rings about 6 mm (¼ inch) thick.
3. Put the string through the centre of the apple rings. Pretend you are stringing beads.
4. Hang the string of apples in the warmest, driest place in your house—in your attic, near the furnace or in the kitchen. (Make sure none of the apple rings touches another.)
5. In one week the apples should be dry. Store them in a glass jar or paper bag. Dried apples make great snacks for a hike.

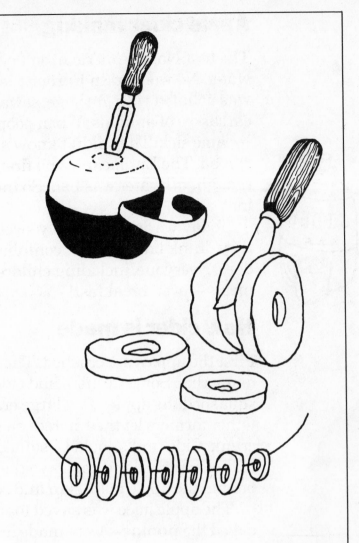

Believe it or not

Yes, it's true...

— that the world's biggest apple pie weighed 13.66 tonnes (30,116 lbs) and took 600 bushels of apples to make. If each person eats 227 gms (8 ounces) of pie how many people did it take to eat the biggest pie in the world?

— that George Adrian of Indianapolis, Indiana, picked 366 bushels of apples in eight hours. Each bushel of apples holds about 45 apples, so how many apples did fast-fingered George pick?

See page 60 for the answers.

Apple cider making

The first North American settlers were afraid to drink the water. No wonder! In Europe the water from rivers and lakes was polluted with garbage, sewage and sometimes the dead carcasses of animals. When people drank this water they became sick. They didn't know about germs or how diseases spread. The Europeans who first settled North America thought *all* water was bad. So they drank wine, beer and cider instead.

Today we drink a bubbly sweet cider, but in pioneer days, they drank hard cider. It contained alcohol like wine and beer does. Everyone, including children, drank hard cider with their meals—even breakfast!

How cider is made

First the apples are crushed. The pioneers had many ways of doing this. Some farmers had cider mills or presses that squashed the apples as a large crank was turned by hand. Other farmers let their horses do the hard work of turning the crank. Cider mills could be squat, tall, round or square, but all of them crushed the apples so the juice squished out leaving behind the apple pulp, skin and seeds.

The apple juice was saved for drinking. The crushed apples, called the **pomace**, were made into cider. First the pomace was put into a huge vat. Every few hours the farmer turned the pomace with a shovel so that the air could mix with it. After being mixed with air for a day, the pomace was shaped into big thick pancakes called "cheeses."

These "cheeses" were stacked high. Between each one there was a layer of straw. The stacks of "cheeses" up to 1 m (3 feet) high were put into a press. Some of the presses looked like gigantic screws. The press was tightened until all the juice from the "cheeses" squished out into a clean barrel. This juice was covered with a loose-fitting lid. The pomace was thrown to the pigs and cows for a special treat. The seeds were saved for planting.

In a few weeks the juice would be bubbling. This is called **fermentation**. It happens when oxygen in the air mixes with the natural fruit sugars in the apple juice. After the cider had fermented, the farmer would "rack off" the juice. Even though the apple peels, core and pulp had already been removed there would still be bits of solids floating in the juice. This is called sediment. The sediment would sink to the bottom of the barrel, and the farmer would scoop the clear juice off the top, leaving the sediment behind. This is called racking off.

The farmer would press the apples in late October, rack off in December and again in February, and the first cider would be ready in June.

Crushing apples in the cider mill

Mixing the pomace with air

Squeezing the juice from the cider "cheeses"

Making cider vinegar

Once the pioneers had cider, it was easy to make cider vinegar. (Vinegar was needed for pickling — another way of preserving fruits and vegetables.)

Cider vinegar is just cider with lots of air in it. When the oxygen in the air mixes with the alcohol in the cider it makes acetic acid. This acid has the vinegary smell you get when you open a new jar of pickles. If you leave a barrel of apple cider open for a couple of months it will turn into cider vinegar.

Sometimes the pioneers didn't want to wait that long. To speed things up, they would hang a barrel of cider over an empty barrel. In between they would put a box filled with wood chips from a birch tree. They would punch a hole in the cider barrel and in the wood chip box. As the cider dripped slowly from the barrel through the wood chips there was time for the air to mix with each drop of cider. By the time the empty barrel was full — in just a few weeks — the vinegar was ready.

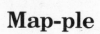

Map-ple

Apples grow in many parts of the United States and Canada. Look at the map to see the largest growing areas in North America. All of these places have exactly what the apple tree needs to grow — lots of sunshine, a little cold weather in winter (not *too* cold), rich, well-drained soil and little wind. Did you know that an apple tree will die if its roots are always wet?

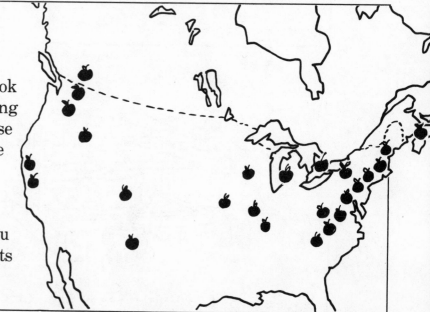

Old apple beliefs

People once believed that:

- if you twisted the stem of an apple and called out the letters of the alphabet with each twist, you could discover the first letter of your true love's name. The name would begin with the letter you called just as the stem broke off from the final twist.

- if there were ripe apples and apple blossoms on the tree at the same time, somebody was going to die.
- if you threw an apple onto the roof of your house and it stayed there, you would have bad luck.
- you could tell the number of children you would have by counting the number of seeds inside your apple.

More pie, please

Take an apple pie. What is the most pieces you can get with four straight cuts? *Answer on page 60.*

The apple tree at work

You are a living breathing thing and so is an apple tree. Can you guess which part of the tree breathes and which part drinks? Do you know that the tree has a backbone and a fluid that acts a lot like blood?

The tree's feet

Your feet give you a firm foundation so you don't tip over. An apple tree has roots for the same reason. But roots do a lot more than feet. They prevent the tree from starving. The roots drink up water from the soil that is rich in **nutrients**. The tree must have this water to grow. The roots have another big job—they store food for the tree during the winter. Roots are so important that if a large root is destroyed, the whole tree could die.

The tree's backbone

The trunk holds the leaves and branches up to the sun. It also takes water and nutrients from the roots up to the leaves. And it takes food made by the leaves down to the roots. The trunk is like an elevator that never stops. You can see how the tree transports food by trying *Mixed-up water* on page 28.

Imagine peeling off layers of tree trunk like you peel off winter clothes. (Don't ever peel off the bark in real life: the tree might die.) Look at the bark. It's rough and cracked. That's because bark stretches as the tree grows. Bark protects the tree from hungry animals and insects. It keeps the tree warm in winter and cool in summer.

Under the bark is a thin inner bark called the **phloem**. Food made by the leaves travels through the phloem to the roots.

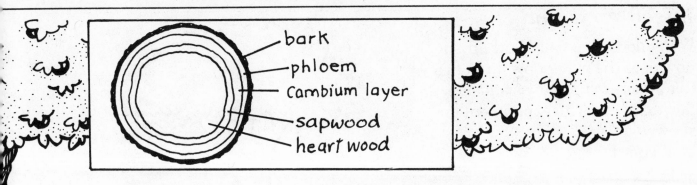

bark
phloem
Cambium layer
sapwood
heart wood

Under the phloem is the **cambium**. You need a microscope to see it. The cambium manufactures the phloem and the woody parts of the tree. It covers the inside of the tree from the tip of the branches to the roots—just as a sleeping bag would cover you from your head to your feet.

Under the cambium are layers of wood. One layer is called **sapwood**. It is a spongy layer that helps carry the water from the roots to the leaves. At the very centre of the tree is the **heartwood**. This wood helps the tree stand upright, a bit like your skeleton holds *you* upright.

The tree's lungs

Leaves breathe, a bit like your lungs do. You can actually see plants breathing. To see for yourself, try *Breathing Plants* on the next page. But leaves also make food. Inside the leaves there is a chemical called **chlorophyll**. When the sun shines on the chlorophyll, the leaf manufactures food from the carbon dioxide in the air and the water inside the plant. While the leaf is making food it breathes out oxygen.

The tree's reproductive system

Future apple tree generations depend on the flowers of the apple tree. The apple flowers, called blossoms, are pale pink and appear in the spring. When they are fertilized with pollen from another flower, an apple seed is "born." Apple seeds can become new apple trees if they are planted in good soil with room to grow roots and have plenty of sunshine, rain and warm weather.

Mixed-up water

Water doesn't usually flow *up,* so how does the water flow up from a tree's roots to the leaves and flowers? Here's an experiment to show you.

You'll need:
a stalk of celery
a knife
two glasses
two different colours of food colouring
a small spoon

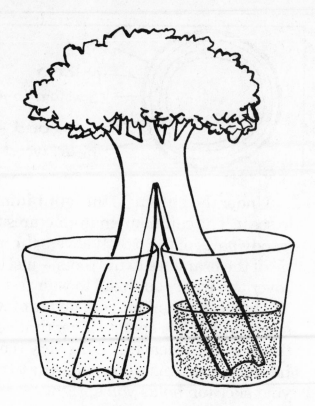

1. Take two glasses and half fill each with water.
2. Mix a spoonful of one food colouring into the water in the first glass and a spoonful of the other food colouring into the water in the second glass.
3. Cut the end off a stalk of celery and split the stalk in half lengthwise—not all the way to the top, just about half way up.
4. Put one part of the stalk in one glass and the other part in the other glass.
5. Wait an hour or two and see what happens.

Inside the celery (and inside the apple tree) there are long, thin tubes. Scientists think that as the water molecules inside the stalk (or trunk) near the top are used by the leaves or evaporate in the hot sun, other water molecules start moving up to fill the empty spaces.

Breathing Plants

When you breathe you make water vapour. Breathe close to a mirror and you'll see. When plants breathe out, they make water vapour too. Put a plastic bag over a house plant and seal it tight. Leave it overnight and see what you find in the morning.

The birth of an apple

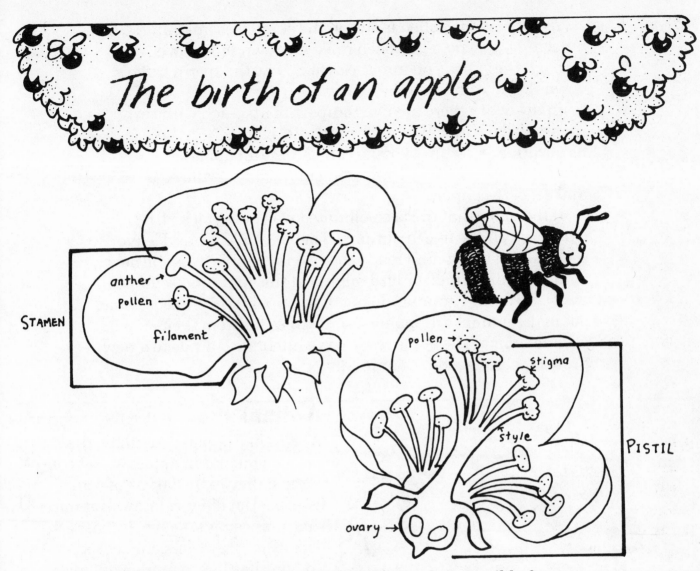

STAMEN

anther →
pollen →
filament →

pollen →
stigma ←
style
ovary →

PISTIL

This bee doesn't know it, but it has just made it possible for an apple blossom to become an apple. The bee has taken the pollen (made mostly of male cells called **sperm**) made by the **stamens** of one apple blossom and left it near the **pistils** (containing the female cells) of another apple blossom. This is called **cross pollination**.

The bee has unknowingly dropped pollen onto the sticky **stigmas** at the top of pistils of the apple blossom. These stigmas are attached to long narrow tubes called **styles** that join deep inside the flower to form a place that looks like a round egg carton. It is called the **ovary**.

As soon as the pollen lands on the stigmas, something amazing happens. The pollen makes its own tube down through the styles and into the ovary. Now the sperm travels down the tube and into the ovary.

In the ovary there are five compartments, each with two eggs called **ovules**. When sperm meets ovule, ZAP!, there is fertilization. A fertilized ovule can become an apple seed. At least one ovule in every compartment must be fertilized to make a perfect apple.

If the apple that the bee pollinated was never picked, it would fall off the tree in autumn. Then it would rot and leave the seeds on the ground ready to grow into apple trees the next spring. Or an animal or bird might eat the apple and scamper away. Birds and animals do not digest apple seeds. Seeds come out in the animal's droppings, sometimes far from their original home. The apple seeds have hitchhiked a ride to a new growing place inside the animal!

Animal apple lovers

Worms like apples. (Actually, the worms you find in apples aren't true worms; they're the larvae of some insects.) But did you know that mice, rats, guinea pigs, squirrels, beavers, deer, bears, raccoons, horses, pigs and gorillas like to munch on apples too?

Wild animals usually eat what is available. Because there aren't many apple trees in the woods, no animal has apples as the most important part of its diet. Still, apples are a nice treat. At most zoos animal apple lovers get to eat apples whenever the fruit is on sale at the market.

Male and female together

Every apple blossom has both male and female parts. The male parts (the stamens) produce the pollen and the female parts (the pistils) receive the pollen and hold the ovules. Some flowers can pollinate themselves; pollen from the stamens goes to the pistils of the same flower. But apple blossoms must be *cross*-pollinated. This means that pollen from one flower must travel to another before fertilization can take place. This is where the bee comes in.

From blossom to apple

Once the apple seeds start growing, the blossom changes
into an apple. First the petals fall to the ground. Then the ovary
starts growing. The ovary has a thin layer that wraps around
the seeds to protect them from bumps and harsh weather.
When you eat an apple you can see this thin layer—it is the
apple core. Next, the outer layers of the ovary swell up like a
balloon and become the eating part of the apple. The **calyx**,
stamens and pistils become the dry, hairy part at the bottom of
the apple.

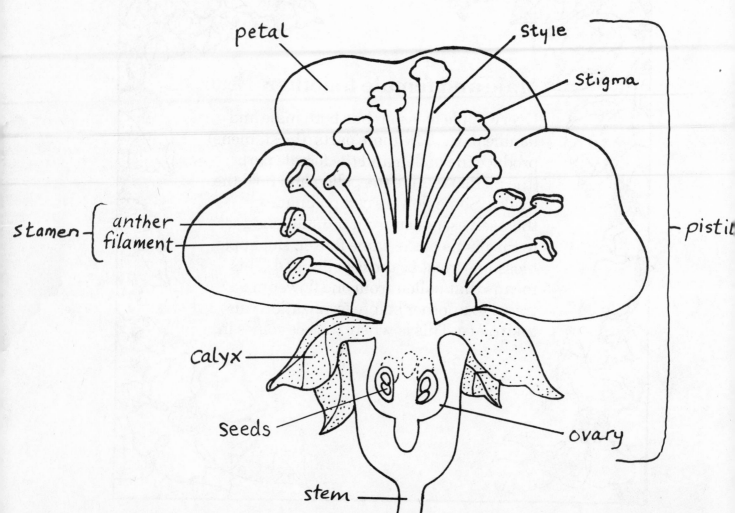

The world's largest apple, found in England, weighed 1.357 kg (3 pounds, 1 ounce). That's almost as heavy as most *bags* of apples.

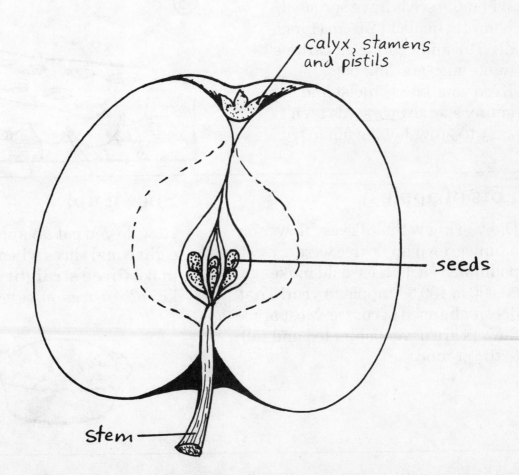

calyx, stamens and pistils

seeds

stem

Growing an apple tree

An apple seed planted today will take fifteen years to produce an apple! If you've got lots of time— and patience—here's how to do it:

1. Trick the apple seeds into thinking they have just gone through a long, cold winter. Put them in the fridge for six weeks.
2. Sprout the seeds by putting them between two pieces of damp blotting paper. (Keep the paper wet all the time and be patient—it might take weeks.)
3. When the seeds have sprouted, plant them about 2.5 cm (1 inch) deep in small pots. Egg cartons make good starting pots.
4. Keep your plants moist and in a sunny spot. Apple seeds aren't easy to grow, but it's fun to try.

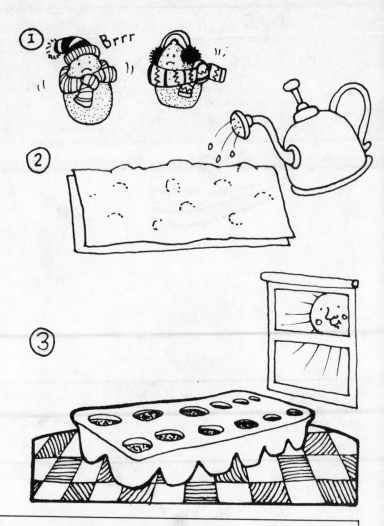

Lots of apples

Did you know that if every flower on a fully grown apple tree were pollinated each tree would make 50,000 to 100,000 apples a year! That doesn't happen of course. Most apple flowers are never pollinated and fall to the ground.

Slice it up!

How do you cut an apple pie into eight equal slices when you can only make **three straight cuts** with a knife? *Answer on page 60.*

Building a better apple

What do you get when you pollinate a McIntosh apple tree with another McIntosh apple tree? McIntosh apples, right? Sorry, wrong. It sounds logical, but an apple tree must be pollinated by a *different* kind of apple tree to make apples. Cross a McIntosh with a McIntosh and you get nothing.

What do you get when you pollinate a McIntosh tree with a Delicious tree? Apples that are red, crunchy and knobby at one end? Maybe. But you might also get an apple that doesn't look like either "parent." There's no way of telling how the fruit will look or taste when you cross two different apple trees. Sometimes the fruit of two trees is better than either parent; sometimes it is worse. To avoid "bad apples," growers have found scientific methods of growing *exactly* the kind of apples and apple trees that they want in their orchards.

How growers make their own trees

Today's apple trees are made just like the monsters in horror stories. Growers take the best parts from different trees and stick them together with glue and tape.

Usually they start with **rootstocks**—roots with a bit of trunk. Rootstocks are grown at special tree farms, and each rootstock comes with information about how high it will grow, how deep its roots will go. This helps growers plan how far apart to plant their trees.

Grafting and budding

Most growers use grafting to attach a fruit-bearing branch of a tree to the rootstock. This is no ordinary branch. It's called a **scion** and it's a short shoot that has three to four buds on it. (Buds become the leaves and blossoms of the apple tree.) The scion is taken from a tree that has the kind of apples the grower wants. The grower sticks the scion into a small slash in the rootstock about 20 cm (8 inches) above the ground. Tape or glue is used to hold the scion and rootstock together.

Sometimes the growers use budding instead of grafting. Budding means taking one bud from a tree and attaching it under the bark of the rootstock with glue or tape.

New trees created by budding and grafting are kept in a protected nursery for a year before they are planted in an orchard.

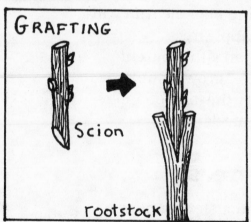

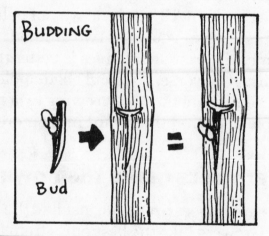

Top heavy!

In the wild, nature makes sure that a tree with lots of big fruit has a large trunk with big roots. This helps ensure that it won't tip over in the wind. But in today's orchards, a grower can bud or graft big fruit-bearing branches onto a short trunk with shallow roots. It means farmers can get more fruit in less space.

Superapple

How would you like
a perfect apple
to taste and to look?
Here are some
of the things growers
want. Which
would you choose
for your superapple?

SKIN COLOURS	INSIDE	OTHER
pink tinge	juicy	long shelf life
delicate red	crisp	low bruising
striped red	sweet	early ripening
bright green	tangy	late ripening
yellowish	tart	pest resistant
streaky red	soft	
pale yellow	mealy	
red blush	white	
light green	firm	

The apple of your choice

Because growers can assemble their own apple trees, they try
to make new, perfect apples. Some growers liked the McIntosh
apple but thought it took too long to ripen. So they crossed the
McIntosh with the Yellow Transparent apple. The result: the
Early McIntosh which looks like a McIntosh but ripens early
like a Yellow Transparent. Growers can make apples with new
tastes and textures, shapes and colours. So far no one has
made a square, sour, purple apple. But then, who would want
one?

Most apples today must travel well, resist bruising, keep
their colour and look terrific because that is what buyers seem
to want. But some people say that the new "superapples" aren't
as tasty as the good old-fashioned apples.

MAKING APPLE DOLLS

Sometimes people call apple dolls "Granny dolls" because of their wrinkled skin. They are as popular today as they were in pioneer days.

You'll need:

a round hard apple without any bruises

small knife

lemon juice concentrate (this comes in a bottle)

6 pipe cleaners

leftover fabric scraps cut into 2.5-cm (1-inch) wide strips

masking tape

two whole cloves

fabric scraps big enough to make doll's clothes

wool yarn or cotton batting

glue

1. Peel the apple, leaving the stem and a circle of peel around the stem. Carve a mouth, nose and eyes into the apple. You don't have to be fancy (remember that great Hallowe'en pumpkin you made last year). Make your cuts pretty deep but don't go all the way through the apple. If you want, you can carve a chin, cheeks and ears.

2. Pour the bottled lemon juice into a bowl. Soak the apple for an hour. The lemon stops the apple from turning brown as it dries.

3. Tie a string to the apple stem. Hang the apple in a warm, dry place. It takes from 15 to 30 days to dry and shrink. (YOU'D BETTER WARN EVERYONE SO THEY DON'T THINK YOU'RE MAKING SHRUNKEN HEADS.)

4. Make the doll body by twisting pipe cleaners together. Bend one pipe cleaner as shown for the body. Cut another pipe cleaner in two. Bend the ends a little bit for hands and attach to the top of the circle for arms. Twist two pipe cleaners onto the bottom of the circle for legs. Cut a 2.5-cm (1-inch) piece of pipe cleaner and twist it onto the top of the circle to make a neck.

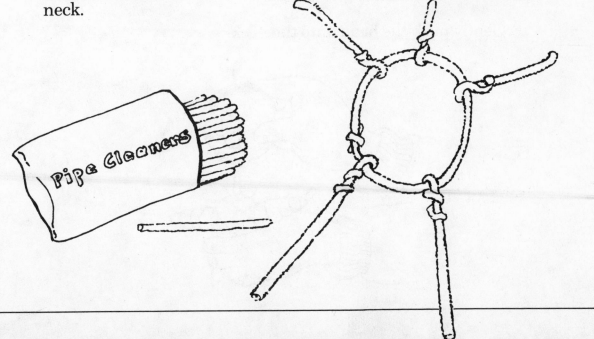

5. Wrap strips of fabric around and around the pipe cleaners until the pipe cleaners are padded into a body. Do not wrap the neck. Now wrap masking tape around the body to keep all the fabric tight.

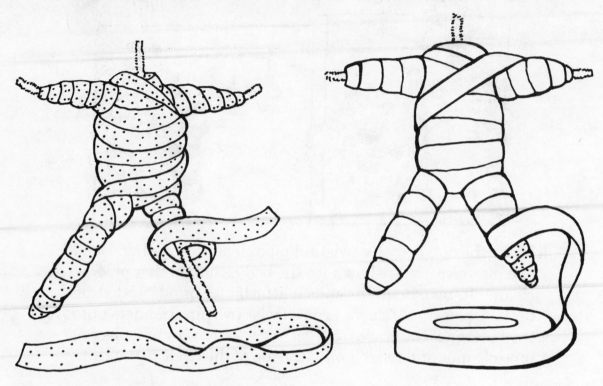

6. Gently push the head onto the neck.

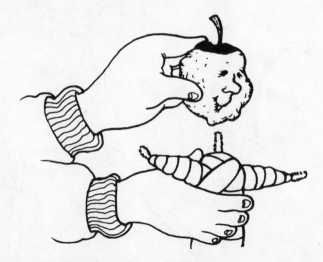

7. Gently pull off the stem. Glue pieces of wool yarn or cotton batting onto the small piece of peel at the top of the apple to make hair. Push cloves into the head for eyes.

8. Use your imagination to make clothes out of the scrap fabric.

Apple printing

Who needs to buy wrapping paper when you can make it?

You'll need:

an apple
knife
tempera paint (any colour)
aluminum pie plate
5 sheets of absorbent paper towel
white or brown paper

1. Cut the apple in half lengthwise.
2. Pour just enough paint into the pie plate to cover the bottom.
3. Make a stamp pad by putting the sheets of paper towel on top of one another and then folding them in half. Put the stamp pad into the pie plate and let it soak up the paint.
4. Press the cut side of the apple down onto your stamp pad so that it becomes coated in paint.
5. Press your apple onto the paper. Don't move it around. Keep repeating your apple print until you get a design you like. Let it dry. Use for wrapping paper.

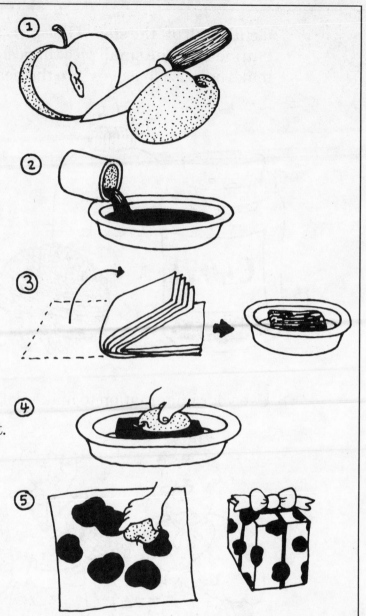

What pests!

Tent caterpillars are apple pests. They eat the apple tree leaves and can destroy the tree. The pioneers didn't have **pesticides** to kill apple pests. Instead, farmers had to shake their trees to loosen the bugs from their nests. Then they would catch the caterpillars in a large net and crush them with a hammer.

In the orchard

Want to find out about apple growing? Ask an expert. Here's Farmer Brown, who has an average-sized orchard of 1,875 trees.

Q: Farmer Brown, why are all your apple trees shaped like pyramids?
A: I cut the branches into this shape. If I didn't the branches would grow willy-nilly all over the place. A lot of the apples would die because they never got any sun. By pruning the trees into this pyramid, all the fruit gets a suntan.

Q: Why do you plant them all in rows and so far apart?
A: Well, the trees need room for their roots to grow and the leaves need sunshine. And I need space to bring a picking truck or pesticide sprayer between the rows.

Q: Why do you need pesticides?
A: Apple trees are plagued by bugs. They get fire blight, apple scab, maggots, bagworms, cankerworms and coddling moths. I check the trees for the little critters. I wait for a still day before I spray—I don't want that stuff blowing all over the place. Sometimes we use bugs to fight the bugs! The enemy bugs hunt down the apple-eating bugs and eat them. The result: some happy bugs and some untouched apples.

Your grandparents might remember apples with names like Rhode Island Greening, Snow and Pippin, but it's hard to find these apples today. Although there are more than 7,000 kinds of apples, most places have local favourites. For example, people from New Jersey like Winesaps, while people from Quebec prefer Lobos. The most popular apples are the Big Six: McIntosh, Golden Delicious, Red Delicious, Spartan, Idared and Northern Spy. Try to match the Big Six with these apple descriptions. *Answers on page 60.*

1 I am a medium- to big-sized apple that is very round. If you know anything about Greek soldiers you might guess my name. I am solid red with tiny white dots on my skin and people like to use me for eating and cooking.

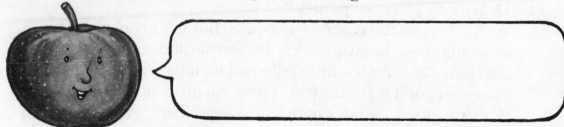

2 Don't be fooled by my name—I'm not a secret agent. I'm a big apple with striped red skin and creamy yellow flesh. Although I'm wonderful baked into pies and sauces, I'm seldom eaten raw.

3 I'm oval, bright yellow, thin-skinned and I have five nobs. My taste is in my name and I'm tastiest when you eat me raw.

4 Sometimes I'm used to make pies or juice, but my claim to fame is my rosy red skin and my wonderful taste. I'm Canada's favourite eating apple.

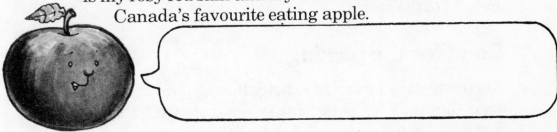

5 My name rhymes with bed and I'm big. My skin is deep red and splattered with greenish-yellow patches. People use me for almost everything — baking, cooking, eating and drinking.

6 If you cook me I don't taste terrific. On the other hand, I am absolutely — oops, almost gave my name away — to eat. I'm oval, bright red and have five knobs at the bottom.

45

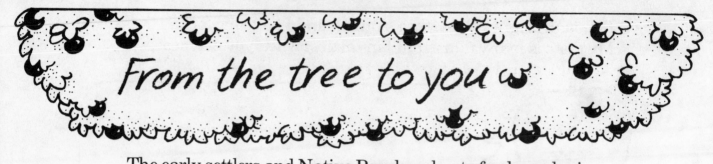

From the tree to you

The early settlers and Native People only ate fresh apples in early winter. From January until August they ate dried or preserved apples. Today, thanks to scientific storage methods, we can eat apples all year round. Here's what happens from the orchard to the store.

Good for the picking

Apples must be picked at exactly the right moment. Picked too soon, they may never become sweet, tasty fruit. Picked too late, they quickly rot.

Farmers pick plump, juicy ripe apples when they want to sell them right away at a market or roadside stand. They pick underripe apples when they want to store their apples or pack them for travelling.

Some farmers can tell whether the apples are ready for picking just by cutting into one. When a Delicious apple is ripe, for example, the inside changes from a greenish colour to white. Other farmers take a bite of the apple. Usually, the sweeter the apple tastes, the riper it is. Many farmers use a calendar to calculate their harvesting times. (Some varieties of apples ripen earlier than others.)

Most farmers use scientific tests to tell when their apples are ready for harvesting. One of the most common tests is the starch test. You can do this yourself by following the instructions in the box on this page.

Picking apples

Most apple orchards stick by the tried-and-true old-fashioned way of picking apples — by hand. Workers gently pluck the fruit from the branches. Some can pick with both hands at once! The important thing is not to bruise or drop the fruit. Once the apples are collected, they are sorted. Bruised fruit are set aside for animal feed, while the good apples go into wooden apple crates.

Some farmers use large, mobile machines to shake the apples off the tree. The apples bruise when they crash to the ground and are used to make juice, cider and applesauce.

The starch test

Some farmers use this simple test to see whether their apples are ripe. You'll need:
brown iodine
a small paint brush
an apple
a knife

1. Cut the apple in half.
2. Brush some brown-coloured iodine onto the cut surface.
3. Watch and you'll see that parts of the apple become a dark purple colour. The purple means there is starch there. If your apple has lots of purple, it has a lot of starch and it is not yet ripe. If your apple has only a bit of purple, it has only a little starch. Most of the starch has already turned to sugar, which is why the apple tastes sweet. It's ripe!

Storing apples

Apple farmers used to store and transport apples in barrels. (Thrifty pioneers would make furniture out of used apple barrels.) Today's farmers use special wooden apple bins that were first designed in British Columbia. These bins are put into the centre of the orchard during picking time. When they are full, they are lifted with a forklift truck and moved to a storage area.

The apples are sorted again to weed out rotten and bruised apples. The good apples are stored as quickly as possible. If an apple sits for just *one day* in 21°C (70°F) weather, it loses *one whole week* of life. Ripe and slightly bruised apples are sold right away.

Half the apples are put into **cold storage** where the temperature is 0°C (32°F). Golden Delicious apples can be put into cold storage for up to seven months, but McIntosh apples will only last for four months. The other half are put into **controlled atmosphere storage.** Here the apples stay fresh for almost a year. They are sealed into an airtight room where the amounts of oxygen and carbon dioxide in the air can be

Then...   Now...

changed. In the orchard, fruit breathes in (inhales) lots of oxygen and breathes out (exhales) carbon dioxide. Scientists know that when they cut down on the oxygen and add more carbon dioxide to the air, it takes the apples longer to ripen. In controlled atmosphere storage the amounts of carbon dioxide and oxygen in the air are controlled so that the apples ripen slowly without losing any flavour. The amount of water in the air (the humidity) is also controlled to keep the apples from shrivelling.

The apples you buy from October to February probably were in cold storage. The apples you buy from February until the next apple harvest probably were stored in controlled atmosphere storage.

To the store

Apples must be graded by size, shape and condition and packed to send to the stores. They travel along a conveyer belt and are judged for size by machines or people. Then the apples are packed into plastic bags with holes so they can breathe, or into baskets. Finally, the apples are loaded onto clean, temperature-controlled trucks so they don't get too hot or too cold on their trip to the store.

Beauty may or may not be skin deep

You can't tell if an apple is ripe just by looking at its skin colour. If there have been cool nights and sunny days late in the growing season, the apples will have a deep colour. But if there were warm nights and cloudy days at the end of the season, the apple will have paler skin.

49

Buying apples

Look for apples without bruises. To keep store-bought apples fresh, keep them in a plastic bag with air holes and put them in the crisper section of the fridge. If you have a basket of apples, cover them with a perforated plastic sheet and keep them in a cool, airy, dark place. When you store apples make sure you don't put them near celery, cabbage, lettuce, carrots, rutabagas, potatoes, fresh paint, fertilizers, dirty hay or straw. Apples will absorb all of these odours and flavours. Yuck!

How to pick an apple

Cup the apple in the palm of one hand. With your other hand put your thumb and forefinger at the base of the apple's stem. Twist very gently so that the apple moves a bit to the side and a bit upward. The stem will snap off the branch.

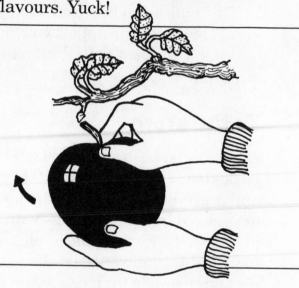

Apples by the bushel

Americans grow about 190 million bushels of apples a year. Canadians produce almost 25 million bushels. Almost three-quarters are sold fresh; the rest are canned, dried, frozen or made into apple juice, cider or vinegar.

An apple a day...

In the old days, a kid with a wart would sneak off to the apple orchard and cut a hole in the bark of an apple tree. When the hole grew over with new bark, the wart was supposed to disappear. And it wasn't just warts that apples were supposed to cure. The pioneers thought apples could cure sunburn, dandruff and stomach aches too. For a long time they thought that an apple a day kept the doctor away. Was it true? Well, apples *are* nutritious and have lots of the fibre we need to keep healthy...but they're not magic health cures.

Actually, it's more likely that an apple a day keeps the *dentist* away. Some people think that an apple is almost as good as a toothbrush for keeping your teeth clean. Biting into an apple and chewing massages your gums and keeps them healthy. All the water and juicy fruit help clear the disease-causing plaque off your teeth. So the next time somebody tells you that an apple a day keeps the doctor away, set them straight.

How to eat an apple

Pick up apple in one hand, open mouth and bite. That's the simplest—and most nutritious—way to eat an apple. A lot of the nutrition in the apple is in the skin. When you peel an apple you lose a half to a third of all the Vitamins A, C and iron. When you cook apples you lose more vitamins and minerals. And when you drink apple juice you get a lot less of Vitamins A and C than when you eat raw apples. That's why many juice companies vitaminize their juice—they put the lost vitamins back into the juice. The most nutritious apple is *au naturel*— raw with the skin on.

Health food

Apples are brimming with minerals such as phosphorus, calcium, iron, sodium, potassium and magnesium. They have Vitamins A, B1, B2, B3, B6, B12, C and E and folic acid. Vitamins and minerals keep your skin, teeth and bones growing and healthy. They are low in cholesterol and fat. And you thought apples just tasted good!

Apple workout

A medium-sized apple has about 75 calories. If you are an average-sized kid it will take you about 35 minutes of swimming or slow bicycling, 2 hours of chess playing, 2 hours of TV watching, and 2½ hours of sleeping to burn off the calories in an apple.

Apple yogurt

Instead of grabbing an apple from the fridge, eat your apples raw in a fruity apple yogurt. This recipe makes enough for one person but you can easily make more by increasing each ingredient.
You'll need:
an apple corer
a knife
a small bowl
a mixing spoon
1 medium apple
a handful of crunchy granola
a handful of raisins, dried apricots or any other fruit you like (how about prunes or dried bananas?)
250 mL   plain yogurt   1 cup

1. Core the apple. Leave the skin on and cut into small pieces. Put the apple into a small bowl.
2. Add the other ingredients. Stir well and enjoy.

On what side of your house should an apple tree grow?

On the outside.

52

Have an apple party

Some months are just plain blah! They have no birthdays, no holidays and crummy weather. So why don't you plan an apple party? You can send apple invitations, decorate with garlands of apples, play apple games, eat apple food and top it all off with some pretty spectacular candy apples.

The invitations

Make your own because it's more fun and a lot cheaper than buying invitations. Take pieces of construction paper and stack them on top of one another. (You'll need as many pieces of paper as guests.) Draw a big apple on the top piece and then cut through all the layers. You could tape an apple seed to the invitation and then use a magic marker to write something like:

This Seed will admit one to the Apple Party on Friday at 1:00 p.m. at 72 McIntosh Way

Drink an apple

If you ever decide to take a walk across a desert you might want to pack some apples. They don't look watery, but each medium apple has 115 thirst-quenching gms (4 ounces) of water.

The food

Try some of the recipes on pages 21, 52 and below, then top the party off with blue candy apples. Remember to make a shopping list before the party so that you can make all the food and have it ready before your friends come.

Applewiches

Who says a sandwich isn't a sandwich unless it's made of bread? Here are some applewiches. You make them with apple slices instead of bread slices.

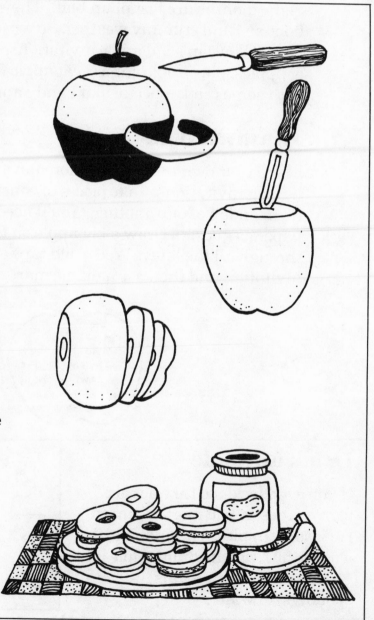

You'll need:
a knife for cutting
an apple corer
a knife for spreading
a cutting board
apples — about one per person
sandwich toppings and fillings such as peanut butter and banana, cream cheese with raisins, cream cheese with cinnamon and honey, liverwurst, tuna salad, egg salad.

1. Slice off the top of the apples at the stem ends.
2. Peel and core the apples
3. Put the apple on its side and carefully cut rings about as thick as bread slices.
4. Make an apple sandwich out of apple rings and filling.

Blue Candy Apples

If you've only seen red candy apples, try this recipe for a colourful change. These candy apples can be green, blue, yellow or even red. The trick is to add food colouring to the syrup. Makes 8 apples.

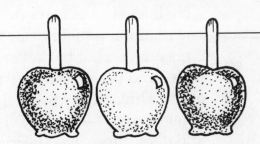

You'll need:
a large cookie sheet
8 Popsicle sticks
a measuring cup
a medium-sized saucepan
a candy thermometer
a wooden spoon
butter or margarine

250 mL	corn syrup	1 cup
250 mL	sugar	1 cup
8	apples	

food colouring — you pick the colour!

1. Grease the cookie sheet with a bit of butter or margarine.
2. Pour the corn syrup and the sugar into the medium-sized pot. Cook over medium heat on the stove. Stir a lot until the syrup starts to bubble.
3. Turn the heat to low and add your food colouring drop by drop until you get the colour you want.
4. Ask an adult to help with the candy thermometer. Dip it into the candy, making sure it doesn't touch the bottom or the sides of the pot. Keep testing with the thermometer until it says: Hard Crack, or 149°C (300°F). This will take 15 minutes or longer.
5. Put the Popsicle sticks into the stem end of the apples.
6. When the candy reaches the hard crack stage, turn off the heat. Ask an adult to help you. Hold the apple by the stick and dip it into the syrup. Put the dipped apples onto the greased cookie sheet. If the syrup hardens before you finish dipping all the apples, turn the heat to low and cook the syrup for a few minutes.

The games

Every party needs games. Here are some old favourites and some new games to try.

Bob for apples

You can play this game inside or outside. If you play outside get a big bucket, or even better, a small plastic wading pool. If you're playing inside, put a big piece of plastic or some garbage bags under a big bucket or tub. Fill the bucket, tub or pool with water and put in as many apples as you have players. The players have to try to catch the apples without touching them. You guessed it—they have to bite the apples. It's wet, it's fun and it's a game that the pioneers used to play.

A is for apple

Everyone sits in a circle. The first person starts the game by saying, "A was an apple and A ate it." The next person says the next letter of the alphabet, B, and then thinks of an object starting with the letter B and an action word beginning with the same letter. He might say, "B was a bat and B borrowed it." The next player says "C" and follows this with an object and then an action word beginning with the letter "C." The player might say, "C was a cat and C captured it." The purpose is to get all the way through the alphabet. It's not very easy when you get to X, Y and Z. This is a thinking game with no winner or losers. If you like, you can make it a contest. Instead of taking turns, each player has a pencil and paper and writes an object and action word for each letter of the alphabet.

Pass the apple

You need at least eight people to play this game. Divide the players into two teams. Each team must stand in a straight line. The player at the start of each team puts an apple under her chin. The idea is to pass the apple to the next player without touching the apple with your hands or letting it drop to the floor. This isn't a game for the ticklish. The players keep passing the apple from one to another until the end of the line. The first team to pass it to the end without touching or dropping it wins. If the apple drops or a player uses his hands to touch it, the apple goes back to the first player and it is passed all the way along again.

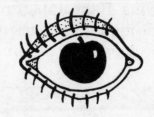

Don't upset the apple cart

This means don't do something that will make you change your plans. People have been saying this for almost 200 years. Why? When a farmer tipped over a cart full of apples on his way to market, he would have to change all his plans for the day because it would take him all day to pick up the apples.

An apple polisher

You wouldn't want to be called an apple polisher. It means someone who tries to "butter-up" a teacher or someone else, even when he or she doesn't like that person. Usually, the apple polisher does it to get away with something. The expression started when schoolboys used to shine an apple they were giving to the teacher. Usually the apple was meant as a bribe to overlook some bad behaviour.

The apple of my eye

This means someone whom you adore. In ancient times people used to call the pupil of their eyes the "apple." Since pupils are essential to seeing, the apple of the eye was very important. Over the years, the expression stopped having anything to do with seeing and instead became a way of expressing love.

One rotten apple spoils the whole barrel

You may have heard this expression, which means that one bad person can influence everyone around him or her. That may or may not be true but it *is* true that one rotten apple can spoil a whole barrel of good apples. That's because rotten apples give off a gas called ethylene. This gas makes fruit ripen more quickly. So apples that would have stayed fresh for a long time quickly turn rotten when they are near a rotten apple.

Apple unscramble

Here are some apple words. Can you unscramble them? *Answers on page 60.*

reoc	lssboom
lpapescuea	dees
eip	radhcro
mtse	recdi
lsciuodies	

Apple writing

You don't need writing paper to send a message to a friend when you have an apple around. To send a message on an apple, you'll need an apple that isn't quite ripe. Ask a fruit farmer early in the fall or the person at your neighbourhood fruit store. Of course, your best bet is to find an unripe apple on a tree. (Ask permission before plucking any fruit.)

Draw your message on paper. Keep it short — maybe just "Hi," or your friend's initials. Cut out each letter of your message. Tape the cut-out letters onto the apple. Now put the apple on a sunny window sill. Put the side with the message towards the sun. When the apple is ripe, peel off the letters. Surprise! Your message is part of the apple.

Believe it or not

It would take 15,058 people to eat the world's biggest pie. George Adrian would have picked 16,470 apples!

More pie, please

The answer is 10. Here's how it's done.

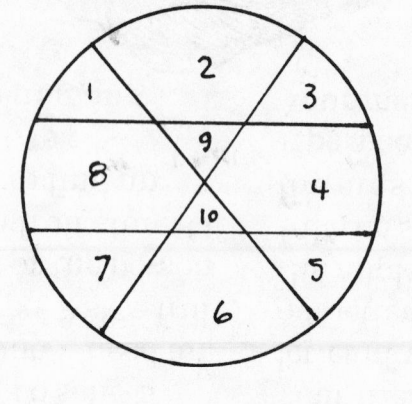

Slice it up!

It's easy when you know this trick. Cut the pie in half. Cut it in half again. That's two straight cuts already. Now stack the pieces one on top of the other. Make your last cut through the middle. Look. You've got eight equal pieces. Just make sure the pieces don't topple.

Who's who in apples

1. Spartan
2. Northern Spy
3. Golden Delicious
4. McIntosh
5. Idared
6. Red Delicious

Apple unscramble

core	blossom
applesauce	seed
pie	orchard
stem	cider
delicious	

No Peeking!

Glossary

Anther   The knobby part of the stamen in the flower. It makes pollen.

Bacteria   Microscopic germs; some cause disease, others cause decay.

Budding   Growers place a bud from one apple tree under the bark of another tree with tape and glue.

Calyx   The cup-like group of leaves that protects the growing bud and later holds the flower.

Cambium   The soft layer of wood deep inside a tree trunk. It produces the woody parts of the tree.

Chlorophyll   The green pigment, or colouring, found in leaves. It traps the energy from the sun so the leaves can make food.

Cold storage   Apples are stored in a room where the temperature is always 0°C (32°F). The cold keeps the apples from ripening too quickly.

Controlled atmosphere storage   Apples are stored in an airtight room where the amounts of oxygen, carbon dioxide and humidity are controlled. This keeps the apples from ripening too quickly.

Cross-pollination   The flowers of one plant are fertilized with the pollen from a different plant.

Fermentation   This occurs when oxygen in the air mixes with the natural fruit sugars in apple juice.

Fertilization   This occurs when male sperm from pollen joins with the female ovules in the ovary to produce a seed.

Fruit   The ripened ovary of the plant that contains the seeds.

Grafting   Attaching one part of a plant to another.

Heartwood   The core of the tree—it helps the tree stand up.

Nutrients   Plants need these to live. They are minerals found in the ground that dissolve in water.

Ovary   The female part of the flower, located at the bottom of the pistils. Inside the ovary are compartments that hold the eggs, or ovules.

Ovules   Tiny eggs that develop into seeds after fertilization.

Pesticides   Chemicals that get rid of insects.

Phloem   A thin layer of bark on the inside of the tree. All of the tree's food (made by the leaves) travels down the phloem to the roots.

Pistils   The female parts of the flower. This includes the stigmas, styles, ovary and ovules.

Pollen   This is powdery and made up mostly of sperm—the male part needed to fertilize an egg. It is made in the anthers of the flower.

Pollinization   This occurs when the pollen from one flower is taken to the stigma of the same flower or another flower. The wind, insects and birds carry the pollen.

Pomace   When an apple is crushed, this is everything that is left but the juice. It includes pulp, seeds, skin and core.

Rootstock   The root and a bit of tree trunk that is especially grown for its size, disease resistance and trunk hardiness. A scion is grafted on to it.

Sapwood   A spongy layer of wood between the bark and the heartwood. It carries water from the roots to the leaves.

Scion   A branch or twig that is grafted onto the rootstock of another plant.

Sepal   The leaves that make up the calyx of a flower.

Sperm   The male cell that joins with the female egg to produce a seed.

Stamens   The male parts of the flower, made up of a knobby anther held up on a thin stalk called a filament.

Stigmas   Sticky knobs in the pistil of the flower. Pollen sticks to them.

Styles   Hollow stalks in the pistil. They widen at the base to form the flower's ovary. Sperm travels down the styles to the ovary.

Index

ALSO IN THIS SERIES:

The Amazing Egg Book
Margaret Griffin and Deborah Seed
Illustrations by Linda Hendry

See how many different animals lay eggs. Dye eggs with cabbage juice and vinegar. Even fry eggs on a sidewalk. Here's another book of experiments, games, crafts, facts, jokes, and recipes— a complete education in eggs!

ISBN 0-201-52334-5

COMING SOON:

The Amazing Paper Book
Paulette Bourgeois
Illustrations by Linda Hendry

Make your own recycled paper. Read all about the first newspaper. Learn the legend of Paul Bunyan, alphabets from around the world, and magic paper tricks. Here's everything you wanted to know about paper, in one fun paperback!

ISBN 0-201-52377-9

Addison-Wesley Publishing Company, Inc.
Route 128
Reading, Massachusetts 01867